## Amazing Archaeology
# King Tut's Tomb

by Julie Murray

Dash!
**LEVELED READERS**
An Imprint of Abdo Zoom • abdobooks.com

# 3 Dash!
## LEVELED READERS

**Level 1 – Beginning**
Short and simple sentences with familiar words or patterns for children who are beginning to understand how letters and sounds go together.

**Level 2 – Emerging**
Longer words and sentences with more complex language patterns for readers who are practicing common words and letter sounds.

**Level 3 – Transitional**
More developed language and vocabulary for readers who are becoming more independent.

THIS BOOK CONTAINS RECYCLED MATERIALS

abdobooks.com

Published by Abdo Zoom, a division of ABDO, PO Box 398166, Minneapolis, Minnesota 55439. Copyright © 2022 by Abdo Consulting Group, Inc. International copyrights reserved in all countries. No part of this book may be reproduced in any form without written permission from the publisher. Dash!™ is a trademark and logo of Abdo Zoom.

Printed in the United States of America, North Mankato, Minnesota.
102021
012022

Photo Credits: AP Images, Getty Images, Granger Collection, iStock, Shutterstock
Production Contributors: Kenny Abdo, Jennie Forsberg, Grace Hansen, John Hansen
Design Contributors: Candice Keimig, Neil Klinepier

## Library of Congress Control Number: 2021940210

## Publisher's Cataloging in Publication Data

Names: Murray, Julie, author.
Title: King Tut's Tomb / by Julie Murray
Description: Minneapolis, Minnesota : Abdo Zoom, 2022 | Series: Amazing archaeology | Includes online resources and index.
Identifiers: ISBN 9781098226640 (lib. bdg.) | ISBN 9781644946374 (pbk.) | ISBN 9781098227487 (ebook) | ISBN 9781098227906 (Read-to-Me ebook)
Subjects: LCSH: Tutankhamen, King of Egypt--Juvenile literature. | Kings and rulers--Tombs--Juvenile literature. | Egypt--Antiquities--Juvenile literature. | Mummies--Juvenile literature. | Excavations (Archaeology)--Juvenile literature. | Archaeology and history--Juvenile literature.
Classification: DDC 932.014--dc23

# Table of Contents

# King Tut's Tomb

King Tut's tomb is one of the most important discoveries in history. His tomb is the only royal grave found intact in modern times.

Tut's tomb is in the **Valley of the Kings**. The valley is located near Luxor, Egypt. It is one of the most famous archaeological sites in the world.

TURKEY

CYPRUS
SYRIA
LEBANON
ISRAEL
JORDAN

LIBYA

EGYPT
King Tut's
Tomb

SAUDI
ARABIA

CHAD

SUDAN

ERITREA

SOUTH SUDAN

# The Boy King

King Tut lived more than 3,000 years ago. He became king when he was about nine years old. This is why he was called the "boy king." Tut ruled from 1333 to 1323 BCE.

Tut was around 19 years old when he died. He most likely died from disease. Some believe a chariot accident caused his death. Others think he may have been killed.

# Finding the Tomb

In 1922, British **archaeologist** Howard Carter discovered the entrance to Tut's tomb. He saw that the outer **chambers** of the tomb had been robbed over the years.

13

In February 1923, Carter's team was able to get into Tut's burial **chamber**. It was untouched. Gold and riches were everywhere.

Ancient Egyptians believed that **pharaohs** should be buried with everything they'd need in the afterlife. So there was much to be found in Tut's tomb.

A **sarcophagus** held three nested coffins. The innermost coffin was made of solid gold. It contained Tut's **mummy**.

Carter and his team spent eight years digging up the tomb. They recorded every item they found. Today, Tut's **mummy** is on display where he was laid to rest thousands of years ago.

# More Facts

- Tut is short for Tutankhaten. It means "living image of Aten." Aten was a sun god.

- More than 5,000 items were found inside the tomb, like chariots, statues, and weapons.

- King Tut's burial mask is made of more than 20 pounds (9.1 kg) of gold. Many believe the mask was made for someone else, not King Tut.

# Glossary

**archaeologist** – a scientist that digs up and then studies objects such as pottery, tools, and buildings. Archaeology is the study of past human life.

**chamber** – a large room.

**mummy** – a dead body that has been preserved with special chemicals and wrapped in cloth. The ancient Egyptians are famous for their mummies.

**pharaoh** – a king of ancient Egypt.

**sarcophagus** – a coffin or container to hold a coffin. Most sarcophagi are made of stone and sit above ground.

**Valley of the Kings** – a place on the west bank of the Nile that holds the royal tombs of many ancient Egyptian kings and queens.

# Index

# Online Resources

**Booklinks**
**NONFICTION NETWORK**
FREE! ONLINE NONFICTION RESOURCES

To learn more about King Tut's Tomb, please visit **abdobooklinks.com** or scan this QR code. These links are routinely monitored and updated to provide the most current information available.